AIR

TWO CAN™

CHANHASSEN, MINNESOTA · LONDON

www.two-canpublishing.com

Published by Two-Can Publishing,
18705 Lake Drive East, Chanhassen, MN 55317

www.two-canpublishing.com

Created by
act-two
346 Old Street
London EC1V 9RB

ISBN 1-85434-907-4

2 4 6 8 10 9 7 5 3

A catalogue record for this book is available from the British Library

Photographic Credits: All photographs are ©Fiona Pragoff, except for the following: Front cover
Pictor International; p.12 (left) NHPA, (top right) Heather Angel/Biofotos, (centre) NHPA; p.13 (top left)
Oxford Scientific Films, (centre left) NHPA; p.14 ZEFA Picture Library (UK) Ltd; p.17 (left) Quadrant
Picture Library, (right) NHPA; p.18 (top) ZEFA Picture Library (UK) Ltd; p.19 (bottom) NHPA; p.20
Oxford Scientific Films; p.21 (top) Ann Ronan Picture Library; p.22 (top) Oxford Scientific Films,
(bottom) Science Photo Library; p.25 Quadrant Picture Library; p.27 (bottom centre) ZEFA Picture
Library (UK) Ltd; p.28 (top) ZEFA Picture Library (UK) Ltd; p.32 (bottom) ZEFA Picture
Library (UK) Ltd; p.33 (top) Oxford Scientific Films, (bottom) NHPA

Thanks to the staff and pupils of St Thomas C.E. Primary School, London W10.

Every effort has been made to acknowledge correctly and contact the source of each
picture and Two-Can Publishing apologises for any unintentional errors or omissions
which will be corrected in future editions of this book.

Printed in Hong Kong by Wing King Tong

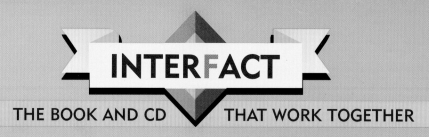

INTERFACT

INTERFACT will have you hooked in minutes –
and that's a fact!

● The disk is packed with interactive games, puzzles, quizzes and activities that are challenging, fun and full of interesting facts.

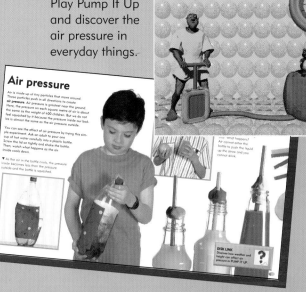

Play Pump It Up and discover the air pressure in everyday things.

● Open the book and discover more fascinating information highlighted with lots of full-colour illustrations and photographs.

Read about simple air experiments you can try at home.

● To make the most of **INTERFACT**, use the book and disk together. Look out for the special signs, called Disk Links and Bookmarks. To find out more, turn to page 40.

40

BOOKMARK

DISK LINK
Guide a hot-air balloon through the crowded skies in ABOVE AND BEYOND!

Once you've clicked on to **INTERFACT**, you'll never look back.

LOAD UP!
Go to **page 39** to find out how to load your disk and click into action.

What's on the disk

HELP SCREEN

Learn how to use the disk in no time at all.

Get to grips with the controls and find out how to use:

- arrow keys
- reading boxes
- 'hot' words

HIGH-FLYER

Take off for your virtual flying test with Winnie Wings!

Fasten your seat belt for a flying test! Learn about aerodynamics, then take the controls of your own virtual aircra that climbs, dives, turns and rolls, just like a real aeroplane!

PUMP IT UP

Can you take the pressure to become a barometer brain?

It's great to inflate!

Find out how weather and altitude affect air pressure with Peter Pumpup. Get the pressure right to help him inflate his mystery objects. It's a gas!

POLLUTION BUSTER

It's an environmental disaster! Only you can save the town.

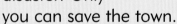

The people of Foulfield need your help. Join the Smog Squad to clean up the town and stop the polluters from taking your breath away.

BOVE
ND
EYOND

Watch out! You're running low on fuel!

he heat
on for a
und-the-world balloon challenge.

tch out, there's a mountain ahead,
d there are storms, skyscrapers and
roplanes to avoid too! Guide your
t-air balloon safely across the sky,
king up air facts along the way.

WIND
SPEED

It's a race
around the
dunes in this
breathless air quiz.

Steer your land yacht to victory in the
race finals! You'll need to brush up on
your air knowledge to steam ahead of
the competition and take the
championship trophy.

OTALLY
UBULAR
UNES

Hello! I'm Andres.

Z X C V B N M

eet the
ndys from
ru and play on their panpipes.

ne up a set of Peruvian panpipes.
the note you need higher or lower?
dres and Andrea will guide you
ong and play a top tune for you!

CATCH
YOUR
BREATH

The gas that pours out of volcanoes is mostly water vapour.

What was
the world
like before it had any air?

Stella has taken a trip back to Earth
four billion years ago, but there's
no air! Click the screen to create the
atmosphere and allow Stella to breathe.

What's in the book

*All words in the text that appear in **bold** can be found in the glossary.*

What is air?

You cannot see or smell ... You can only feel it when ... moves quickly as wind. Yet air is all around us.

Try these experiments to find out more about air. Blow up two balloons an... hang them from a strip ... wood as shown. Tie the wood to the back of a ch... with a piece of thread. Then carefully make a ti... hole in one of the balloo... with a pin. This will let th... air out slowly.

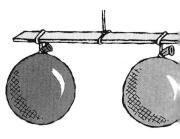

Watch what happens to your scales. Which **weigh...** more, an empty balloon or a balloon full of air? The air in a medium-size... room weighs about as much as you do.

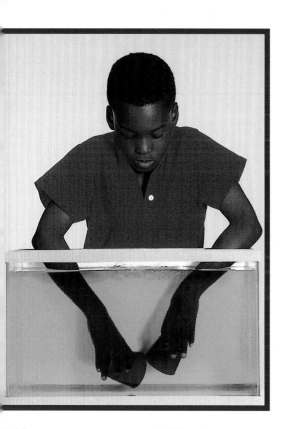

▲ You can even pour air! Fill a large plastic tank with water. Place your beaker upside-down in the water, trapping the air inside it. Now pour the air into the other beaker. Try not to make any air bubbles!

▲ When you breathe in, you take air into your lungs. How much air do you think your lungs can hold? You can measure how much air fills your lungs by blowing through a plastic tube into a measuring jug held upside-down in a tank of water. Try it. You will be surprised how much air you can breathe in and out.

◄ Candles need air to allow them to burn. Ask an adult to light two candles for you. Put a large jar over one candle and a small jar over the other one. Which candle goes out first?

Air pressure

Air is made up of tiny particles that move around. These particles push in all directions to create **air pressure**. Air pressure is greatest near the ground. Here, the pressure on each square metre of air is about the same as the weight of 400 children. But we do not feel squashed by it because the pressure inside our bodies is almost the same as the air pressure outside.

You can see the effect of air pressure by trying this simple experiment. Ask an adult to pour one cup of hot water carefully into a plastic bottle. Screw the lid on tightly and shake the bottle. Then, watch what happens as the air inside cools down.

▼ As the air in the bottle cools, the pressure inside becomes less than the pressure outside and the bottle is squashed.

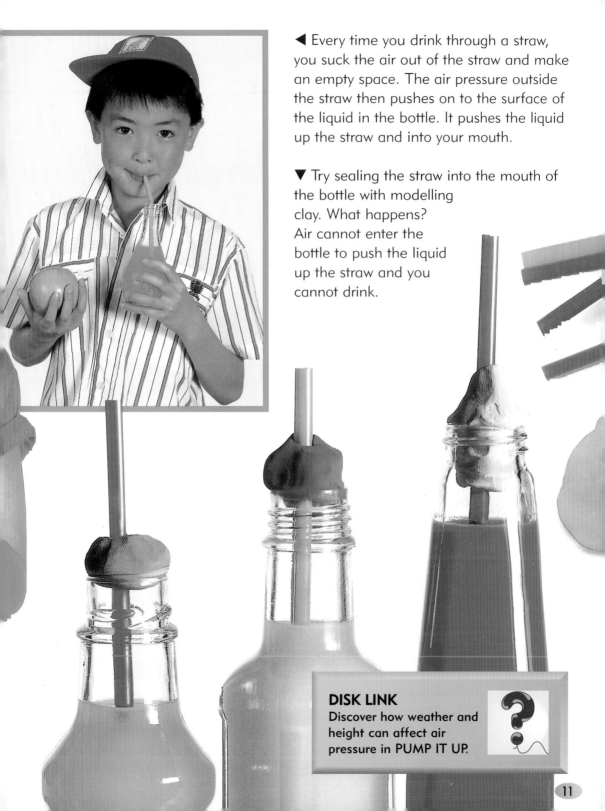

◄ Every time you drink through a straw, you suck the air out of the straw and make an empty space. The air pressure outside the straw then pushes on to the surface of the liquid in the bottle. It pushes the liquid up the straw and into your mouth.

▼ Try sealing the straw into the mouth of the bottle with modelling clay. What happens? Air cannot enter the bottle to push the liquid up the straw and you cannot drink.

DISK LINK
Discover how weather and height can affect air pressure in PUMP IT UP.

Flying seeds

When a plant makes seeds, it spreads them as far as possible to make new plants grow. Different kinds of seeds spread in different ways.

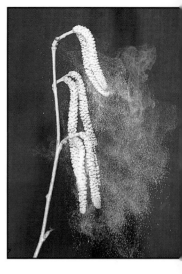

▲ Some plants, such as these catkins, release tiny grains called **pollen**. The pollen is blown by the wind from plant to plant or carried by insects and birds. When the pollen reaches a new plant, new seeds can grow. When there is a lot of pollen in the air, it makes many people sneeze over and over again. This is called hayfever.

◀ Air is an important way of scattering seeds. Many seeds are extremely small and light so they can be carried far away by the wind. These dandelion seeds have feathery strands that act like a **parachute** to help them lift up and travel long distances.

A sycamore tree has seeds shaped like the blades of a **helicopter**. When the seeds fall from the branches, they spin slowly to the ground. Often, they travel far away from the tree. Do you have a sycamore tree in your area?

▼ Make your own sycamore helicopter. Cut out this shape from paper. Fold in the bottom two flaps and weight them with a paper clip. Throw the sycamore helicopter into the air and see what happens.

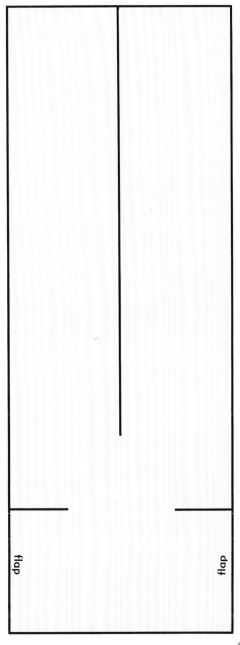

flap

flap

Parachutes

When **sky-divers** jump out of aeroplanes, they use **parachutes** to slow down for a safe landing. As **gravity** pulls each sky-diver towards the ground, the parachute rubs against the air and is slowed down by a force called **air resistance**. Never try to jump from a great height yourself: it is extremely dangerous.

Large crates of supplies are often parachuted out of aeroplanes in places where it is too difficult to land. The larger the parachute, the greater the air resistance and the slower the crate falls. If the parachute is too big, the crate may drift in the air and land in the wrong place.

◀ When a space module returns from the Moon to Earth, it uses parachutes to slow its descent into the ocean.

▼ Ask an adult to help make a parachute out of tissue paper following this pattern.

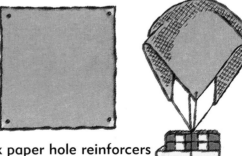

Fix paper hole reinforcers over the holes in the four corners of the parachute. Knot thread through the holes and attach it to a toy truck. Now try out your parachute. If you cut a hole in the centre of the parachute, what happens? Is it easier to hit a target?

Fabulous flying machines

Can a sheet of paper fly?
Of course it can. But it
must be the right
shape so that it can
cut through the air.

DISK LINK
Take a flying
test for your
virtual pilot's
licence in
HIGH-FLYER.

Start with a rectangular sheet of paper and fold it into a dart shape as shown. If you fold flaps at the end of the wings, you can control the path of the dart. Can you make the dart turn to the right? As the air moves past the flaps, it pushes on the dart, changing its direction.

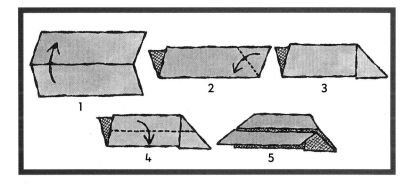

An aeroplane has a **streamlined** shape just like a paper dart but it also has an **engine** to push it along. The top of an aeroplane's wings are curved while the bottom surfaces are flatter. As an aeroplane moves, this special shape creates a change in **air pressure** around the wings and produces a lifting force which pushes the aeroplane up into the sky. Birds, such as gulls, fly in a similar way.

◀ Glue pieces of thread to two ping-pong balls and hang them about 5 cm apart from the back of a chair. Ask a friend if she can move the two balls together without touching them. Can you think how to do it using moving air? All you have to do is blow between the balls and they will move together. Try it!

Hot air rising

Warm air is lighter than cold air. Just like a bubble of air floating to the surface in water, warm air rises. Indoors, warm air cools when it reaches the ceiling, then sinks down again.

▼ You can use rising air to power a spinning snake. Copy this shape on to thin card and cut it out. Ask an adult to fix a pencil on top of a hot radiator with a bit of modelling clay. Then balance the snake on top.

As the air next to the
radiator heats up, it begins
to rise and make the snake
turn around.

DISK LINK
See how hot
air rising can
be used for
transport in
ABOVE AND BEYOND!
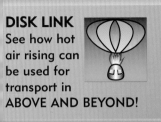

Put your hand just below a
radiator, then above. The
air above the radiator is
warmer because hot air
has moved upwards.

◀ Hang-gliders use rising
air to stay up in the sky.
They do not have **engines**,
so they must find a
column of hot, rising air,
called a thermal, to stay
up. Do you think gliding
would be easier on a hot
day or a cold day? Have
you ever watched hang-
gliders? They find a high
hill where they can launch
themselves into the air
and where the warm
thermals keep them
gliding for a long time.
The pilot hangs from a
harness and steers the
glider with a control bar.

Trapping air to keep warm

Have you ever noticed how a pot of tea goes cold if it is left for a while? Where do you think the heat goes? It is taken away by air currents moving past the pot. Can you think how to stop the air currents?

▲ When a person is cooking in a kitchen, you can sometimes see **steam** rising into the air from hot water in a saucepan. Do you think the steam could be taking heat away with it? What do you think would happen if you place a lid on the saucepan? Would it keep the water hot for longer?

◀ In a few countries, it is extremely cold. To keep warm, people have to stop heat escaping from their bodies. They wear special clothes that trap a layer of air next to their skin. This stops the warm air from escaping and taking the heat with it.

Animals must keep warm as well. These polar bears live in places where there is lots of snow and ice. They grow several layers of thick fur to trap air next to their skin.

➤ Ducks spend much of their time in cold water. They have waterproof feathers on the outside to keep out the water and fluffy feathers close to their bodies to keep in the warm air. Ducks spend a lot of time looking after their feathers to keep them in good condition.

Hot-air balloons

About 200 years ago in France, the Montgolfier brothers noticed that smoke and **steam** move upwards. They thought that if they could trap hot air in a large balloon, it should be able to fly.

In September 1783, the ontgolfier brothers made huge balloon out of a ht material and carefully arted a fire underneath it. person had flown fore, so the first ssengers of the **hot-air** **lloon** were a sheep, a icken and a duck. The st flight was a great ccess, except that the eep trod on the chicken! ne month later, a enchman, Jean François âtre, was the first person go up in a balloon.

Make your own hot-air alloon. Ask an adult to cut it six shapes like this from sue paper. Carefully glue em together along the des, leaving the bottom ges open.

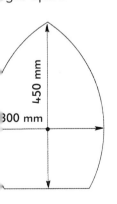

Now ask an adult to fill the balloon with hot r from a hair drier and watch what happens.

Wind power

When the Sun shines, it heats up the land and the air above. The hot air the rises. Cold air rushes in take the place of the ho air. We call this wind. Wi is an extremely strong a current, but there are smaller movements in th air as well, rather like sl and fast-moving current in sea water.

On a windy day, you co see the air moving the leaves and branches on trees and feel it tugging your clothes. The wind h a lot of **energy** and this energy can be used to d useful things.

◄ For centuries, people have used windmills to pump water and grind grain. This modern windfarm has rows of windmills to turn the winc energy into electricity for the local community.

You can have great fun using wind energy to power races with your friends. Make model land yachts like these out of old toy cars, modelling clay and straws. Use thin card for the sails. Experiment with sails of different sizes and shapes. Which sails make the land yachts go fastest?

▶ See if a land yacht moves faster still when you blow on the sail through a straw. Try moving the yacht by blowing gusts of air from a fan on to the sail. Which way works best?

DISK LINK
Race in the land yacht championships in the air quiz WIND SPEED.

Putting out the fire

Air is a mixture of different **gases**. One of these gases is **oxygen**. When a material burns, it needs oxygen. If there is not enough oxygen, the fire will go out.

▼ Here is a trick that puts out a candle flame, as if by magic. You will need a deep bowl, a short candle, vinegar and bicarbonate of soda. Fix the candle in the centre of the bowl and sprinkle about one tablespoon of bicarbonate of soda around it. Ask an adult to light the candle.

Never light a fire or use matches without an adult present.

How can you put out the candle withou blowing on the flame? It's simple: just pour a small amount of vinegar on to the bicarbonate of soda and watch.

As soon as the vinegar touches the bicarbonate of soda it suddenly foams and gives off a gas that puts out the fire. You cannot see the gas but it is heavier than air, so it slowly fills the bowl, instead of floating away. As soon as the gas reaches the candle flame, the light is put out.

he gas that you have made
another gas found in the
r called **carbon dioxide**.
hese trainee **firefighters** are
arning how to use carbon
oxide foam to put out a fire.

DISK LINK
Learn more
about the
mix of gases
in the air in
CATCH YOUR BREATH.

Sounds fun

When you tap an object, such as a drum, its surface quivers and releases fast shaking movements called **vibrations**. You cannot see the vibrations, but they travel through the air to your ears, where you hear them as sounds.

▶ Make a cone from thick paper. Ask a friend to shout from the other side of the garden. Can you hear best with the narrow end to your ear or the wide end?

▲ Tie a spoon to a length of string and hold the ends of the string in your ears. Give another spoon to a friend and ask her to tap your spoon. What can you hear through the string?

▲ Ask an adult to make holes in the bottoms of two yoghurt pots. Push a length of string through the holes and knot the ends. Ask a friend to hold one pot and walk away from her, pulling the string tight. Place your pot next to your ear and ask your friend to speak into the other pot. You now have a mobile phone!

◄ Hold a balloon filled with water next to your ear. Ask a friend to place a ticking watch against the balloon. Can you hear the ticking through the water?

▼ Strike a triangle to make a loud ringing sound. What happens if you touch the triangle?

◄ Have you ever noticed that you see lightning before you hear thunder? This is because light travels faster through the air than sound. You can work out how far away the lightning is. When you see a flash of lightning, count the seconds until you hear the bang from the thunder. Divide by three and you have the distance in kilometres.

Making music

It's easy to make a few simple instruments. Then you can form a band with your friends!

▶ Glue a piece of brown paper tightly over a box. Then hit the box with a wooden stick or a ruler. It sounds just like a drum. Make a set of big and little drums. Can you place them in order of high and low sounds?

▼ Take a wooden ruler and hold it over the edge of a table as shown. When you twang the ruler, it **vibrates** and makes a **note**. Now move the ruler back towards the table and twang it again. Do you notice how the note changes?

▼ You can use two large saucepan lids to make a pair of clashing cymbals. Or hang one saucepan lid from a string and hit it with a ruler.

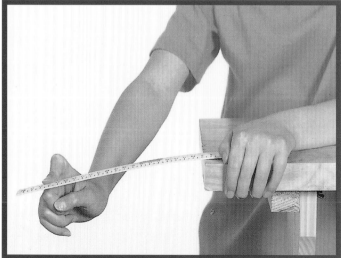

ere are some more instruments to make.

Fill several glass bottles with water. ently tap the side of each bottle to make note. You can make different notes by nanging the depth of the water in the bottles.

Fold a piece of acing paper over comb. Touch the mb gently with your s and hum a tune. his might make your s tickle! Make up fferent tunes to play ongside your friends the drums and mbals.

▼ To make a set of panpipes, ask an adult to cut an old hose-pipe to different lengths. Glue or tape the pipes together on a piece of card in order of size. Close one end of each pipe with thin card. Now blow across the top of each pipe to make a whistling sound. Which pipe makes the highest sound?

▼ To make your own guitar, you need a long, thin box. Glue a thick piece of card across the width of the box and stretch elastic bands of different thicknesses along its length, so that they rest on the card. When you pluck the elastic bands, they vibrate and make a noise. The thick elastic bands make lower notes than the thin elastic bands.

DISK LINK
Tune up and play a set of panpipes in TOTALLY TUBULAR TUNES.

Clean up

When fuels are used in car **engines**, or factories and power plants, they make **chemicals** that are released into the air. Different kinds of paints and sprays also release chemicals. Some chemicals are harmless, but others damage the **environment**. When harmful chemicals mix with the air, they cause **pollution**.

▲ Much of the smoke that pours out of factory chimneys is made up of **steam**, but sometimes it is mixed with polluting **gases**.

◀ When the gases from car **exhausts** mix with particular chemicals in the air, they make an unpleasant fog called **smog**.

Gases can often be cleaned before they reach the air. In many countries, cars are fitted with **catalytic converters** and factories and power plants often use filters to clean the gases they release. We can also help to reduce pollution by cutting back on car use.

Bicycles are a clean and healthy form of transport. Fewer car journeys reduces the amount of air pollution.

DISK LINK
Join the Smog Squad and clean up the air in **POLLUTION BUSTER**.

Fuels, paints and sprays are being developed to give off fewer dangerous chemicals. Many cars now run on cleaner unleaded petrol, and it is also possible to power cars with electricity, gas or fuels made from the natural oils of plants.

True or False?

Which of these facts are true and which are false?
If you have read the book carefully, you will know the answers!

1. A polar bear has several layers of fur to trap air next to its skin.

2. The first hot-air balloon had three passengers. They were a duck, a sheep and a chicken.

3. Catalytic converters are fitted to pet cats to stop them from breathing in polluted air.

4. Wind is caused by cold air rushing in to take the place of hot air.

5. When there is a lot of pollen in the air, many people catch a cold.

6. Hang-gliders use rising air to stay up in the sky.

7. Air is made up of one gas.

8. When you fill glass bottles with different amounts of water, you can make different notes.

9. Smog is made when vehicle exhaust gases mix with chemicals in the air.

10. When a parachute falls through the air, it is slowed down by air pressure.

ANSWERS: 1.T 2.T 3.F 4.T 5.F 6.T 7.F 8.T 9.T 10.F

Air word search

Photocopy this page and see if you can solve this air word puzzle. All of the words listed below can be found either forwards, backwards or diagonally. When you find a word, cross it off from the list.

C	I	T	N	E	M	N	O	R	I	V	N	E	N
T	A	T	N	E	R	R	U	C	R	I	A	P	O
A	I	R	P	R	E	S	S	U	R	E	W	A	O
I	Z	H	B	R	E	A	T	H	E	I	N	R	L
S	H	I	E	O	X	Y	G	E	N	G	T	A	L
E	E	G	L	U	N	G	S	D	E	N	I	C	A
L	M	E	A	M	O	D	M	T	O	M	S	H	B
T	U	P	P	S	G	I	I	A	E	P	P	U	R
E	A	I	L	M	L	T	H	O	H	A	I	T	I
F	L	T	X	L	I	Y	E	R	X	O	M	E	A
G	O	M	S	S	M	O	K	E	W	I	L	W	T
R	A	E	N	A	L	P	O	R	E	A	D	P	O
P	O	L	L	U	T	I	O	N	A	E	R	E	H

aeroplane	carbon dioxide	lungs	smog
air pressure	environment	oxygen	smoke
air current	gas	parachute	steam
breathe	hot-air balloon	pollution	windmill

35

Glossary

Air pressure A force created when air particles push or press against something.

Air resistance A force felt by an object moving through air. Air resistance acts against the moving object.

Carbon dioxide A gas in the air that plants use to make food, and that is used to put out certain kinds of fires.

Catalytic converter A device fitted to a vehicle that reduces the amount of poisonous chemicals released from its engine.

Chemical A solid, liquid or gas that acts and reacts with other substances.

Energy The power to move or work. Wind energy can be used by windmills to make electricity.

Engine The part of a machine that gives it the power to work.

Environment The area where people, plants or animals live.

Exhaust A pipe which releases waste gases from a vehicle into the air.

Firefighter A person trained to put out fires as a job.

Gas A substance that has no shape. Some gases, such as water vapour, can change form and become a liquid or a solid.

Gravity A force which pulls objects together. Earth's gravity pulls everything towards the ground.

Helicopter A machine that uses rotating blades to help it to fly.

Hot-air balloon A giant balloon filled with hot air that can carry people. Hot air is lighter than cool air, so the balloon lifts.

Note A single musical sound.

Oxygen A gas in the air that humans and most animals need to live.

Parachute A large piece of fabric used by sky-divers to slow their descent.

Sky-diver A person who jumps out of an aeroplane, wearing a parachute.

Smog A fog produced when polluting chemicals mix with the air.

Steam Small water droplets in the air.

Streamlined Shaped to travel smoothly through liquid or air. An aeroplane has a streamlined shape.

Pollen Tiny grains, often carried by air, which plants need to reproduce.

Pollution Substances released into the air, sea or land which cause damage.

Vibration A very fast shaking movement.

Weigh To measure how heavy something is.

Loading your INTERFACT disk

INTERFACT is easy to load.
But, before you begin,
quickly run through
the checklist on the
opposite page to
ensure that your
computer is ready
to run the program.

Your INTERFACT
CD-ROM will run on
both PCs with Windows
and on Apple Macs. To make
sure that your computer meets
the system requirements, check the list below.

SYSTEM REQUIREMENTS

PC
- 486DX2/66Mhz Processor
- Windows 3.1, 3.11, 95, 98 (or later)
- 8Mb RAM (16Mb recommended for Windows 95 and 24Mb recommended for Windows 98)
- VGA colour monitor
- SoundBlaster-compatible soundcard

APPLE MACINTOSH
- 68020 processor
- system 7.0 (or later)
- 16Mb of RAM

LOADING INSTRUCTIONS

You can run INTERFACT from the disk – you don't need to install it on your hard drive.

PC WITH WINDOWS 95 OR 98

The program should start automatically when you put the disk in the CD drive. If it does not, follow these instructions.

1 Put the disk in the CD drive
2 Open MY COMPUTER
3 Double-click on the CD drive icon
4 Double-click on the icon called AIR

PC WITH WINDOWS 3.1 OR 3.11

1 Put the disk in the CD drive
2 Select RUN from the FILE menu in the PROGRAM MANAGER
3 Type D:\AIR (Where D is the letter of your CD drive)
4 Press the RETURN key

APPLE MACINTOSH

1 Put the disk in the CD drive
2 Double click on the INTERFACT icon
3 Double click on the icon called AIR

CHECKLIST

● Firstly, make sure that your computer and monitor meet the system requirements as set out on page 38.

● Ensure that your computer, monitor and CD-ROM drive are all switched on and working normally.

● It is important that you do not have any other applications, such as wordprocessors, running. Before starting INTERFACT quit all other applications.

● Make sure that any screen savers have been switched off.

● If you are running INTERFACT on a PC with Windows 3.1 or 3.11, make sure that you type in the correct instructions when loading the disk, using a colon (:) not a semi-colon (;) and a back slash (\) not a forward slash (/). Also, do not use any other punctuation or put any spaces between letters.

How to use INTERFACT

INTERFACT is easy to use.
First find out how to load the program
(see page 39), then read these simple
instructions and dive in!

There are seven different features to explore. Use the controls on the right-hand side of the screen to select the one you want to play. You will see that the main area of the screen changes as you click on to different features.

For example, this is what your screen will look like when you pla ABOVE AND BEYOND, a game where you guide a hot-air balloon across the sky. Once you've selected a feature, click on the main screen to start playing.

Click here select the feature you want to pla

Click on the arrow keys to scroll through the different features or the disk or find your wa to the exit.

Click here to hear the text read out.

DISK LINKS

When you read the book, you'll come across Disk Links. These show you where to find activities on the disk that relate to the page you are reading. Use the arrow keys to find the icon on screen that matches the one in the Disk Link.

DISK LINK
Discover how height and weather can affect air pressure in PUMP IT UP.

BOOKMARKS

As you play the features on the disk, you'll bump into Bookmarks. These show you where to look in the book for more information about the topic on screen. Just turn to the page of the book shown in the Bookmark.

ACTIVITIES

There are activities throughout this book, and on pages 34-35, that you can photocopy and fill in.

HOT DISK TIPS

● If you need help finding your way around the disk, click on the [?] icon to go to the HELP section.

● Any words that appear on screen in a different colour and are underlined are 'hot'. This means that you can touch them with the cursor for more information or an explanation of the word.

● Keep a close eye on the cursor. When it changes from an arrow ↑ to a hand ☝ click your mouse and something will happen.

● After you have chosen the feature you want to play, remember to move the cursor from the icon to the main screen before clicking your mouse again.

Troubleshooting

If you have a problem with your INTERFACT disk, you should find the solution here. You can also e-mail for help at helpline@two-canpublishing.com

YOUR COMPUTER SETUP

RESETTING SCREEN RESOLUTION

Resetting screen resolution in Windows 95 or 98:
Click on START at the bottom left of your screen, then click on SETTINGS, then CONTROL PANEL, then double-click on DISPLAY. Click on the SETTINGS tab at the top. Reset the Desktop area (or Display area) to 640 x 480 pixels and choose 256 colours, then click APPLY. You may need to restart your computer after changing display settings.

Resetting screen resolution for Apple Macintosh:
Click on the Apple symbol at the top left of your screen to access APPLE MENU ITEMS. Select CONTROL PANELS, then MONITORS (or MONITORS AND SOUND), then set the resolution to 640 x 480 and choose 256 colours. Screen resolutions can also be reset by clicking on the chequerboard symbol on the Control Strip.

ADJUSTING VIRTUAL MEMORY

Adjusting the Virtual Memory in Windows 95 or 98:
It is not recommended that these settings are adjusted as Windows will automatically configure your system as required.

Adjusting the Virtual Memory on Apple Macintosh:
If you have 16Mb of RAM or more, AIR will run faster. If you do not have this amount of RAM free, hard disk memory can be used by switching on VIRTUAL MEMORY. Select the APPLE MENU, CONTROL PANELS, then select MEMORY. Switch on VIRTUAL MEMORY. Set the amount of memory you require, then restart your machine.

COMMON PROBLEMS

 Disk will not run
There is not enough memory
available. Quit all other
applications and programs. If this does not
work, increase your machine's RAM by
adjusting the Virtual Memory (see left).

 **There is no sound
(Try each of the following)**

1. Ensure that your speakers or headphones
are connected to the speaker outlet at the
back of your computer. Make sure they are
not plugged into the audio socket next to
the CD-ROM drive at the front of the
computer.

2. Ensure that the volume control is turned
up (on your external speakers and by using
internal volume control).

3. (PCs only) Your soundcard is not
SoundBlaster compatible. To make your
settings SoundBlaster compatible, see your
soundcard manual for more information.

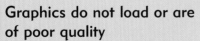 **Graphics do not load or are
of poor quality**
Not enough memory is available
or you have the wrong display setting.
Either quit other applications and programs
or make sure that your monitor control is
set to 256 colours.

 **Graphics freeze or text
boxes appear blank
(Windows 95 or 98 only)**
Graphics card acceleration is too high.
Right-click your mouse on MY COMPUTER.
Click on PROPERTIES, then
PERFORMANCE, then GRAPHICS.
Reset the hardware acceleration slider to
'None'. Click OK. Restart your computer.

 **Text does not fit into boxes
or hot words do not work
(PCs only)**
The standard fonts on your computer have
been moved or deleted. You will need to re-
install the standard fonts for your computer.
PC users require Arial. Please see your
computer manual for further information.

 **Print-outs are not centred
on the page or are partly
cut off**
Make sure that the page layout is set to
'Landscape' in the Print dialogue box.

 Your machine freezes
There is not enough memory
available. Either quit other
applications and programs or increase your
machine's RAM by adjusting the Virtual
Memory (see left).

Index

Work book

Photocopy this sheet and use it to make your own notes.

Work book

Photocopy this sheet and use it to make your own notes.